Guitar Tabsongs Classic Rock

- **14 Rock Classics**

- **Easy Arrangements for Fingerstyle Guitar**

- **Standard Notation and Tablature**

The guitar used on the back cover appears courtesy of John Buscarino.

1 2 3 4 5 6 7 8 9 0

Visit us on the Web at www.melbay.com — E-mail us at email@melbay.com

Contents

Both Sides Now

Words and Music
by Joni Mitchell
arranged for guitar by Ole Halen

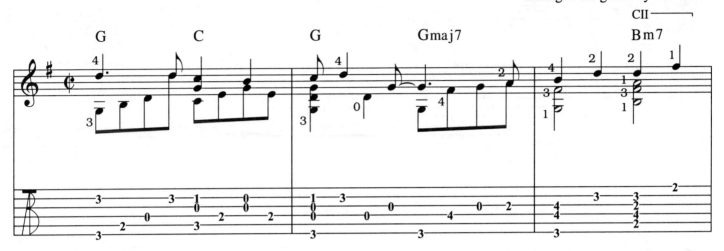

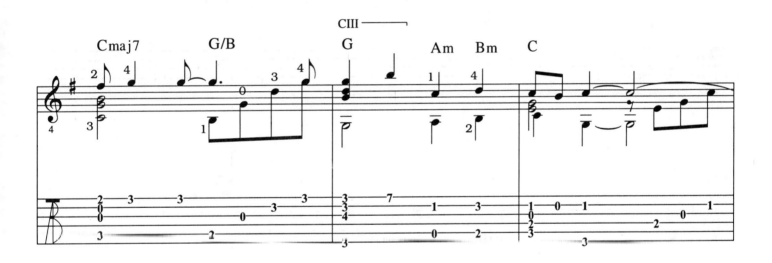

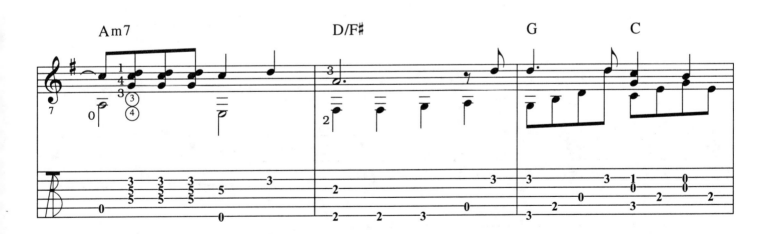

4

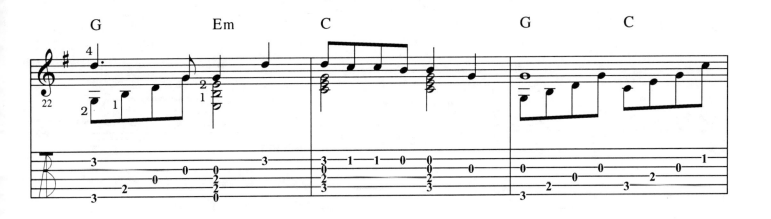

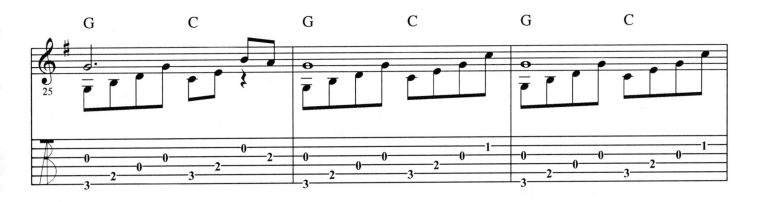

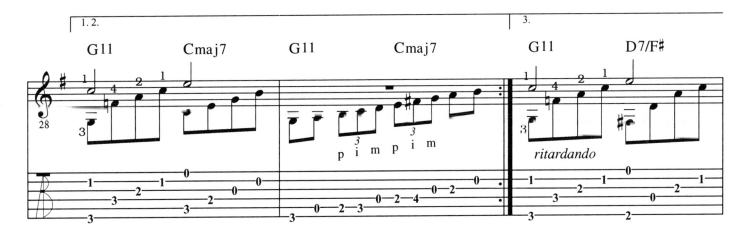

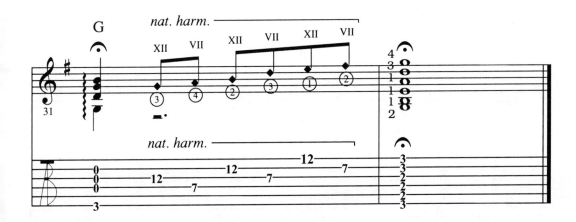

5

Lyin' Eyes

Words and Music by
Don Henley and Glenn Frey
arranged for guitar by Steve Eckels

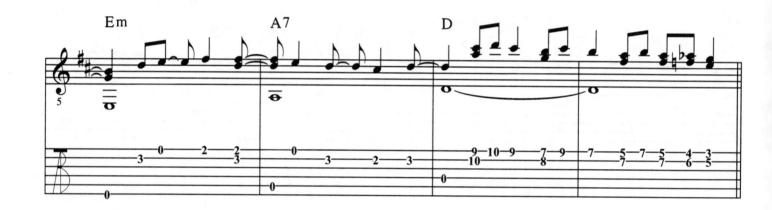

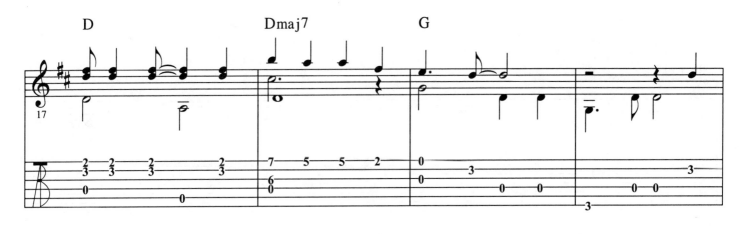

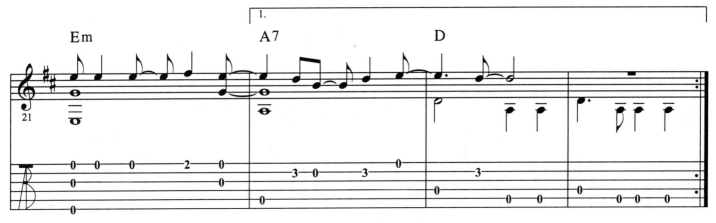

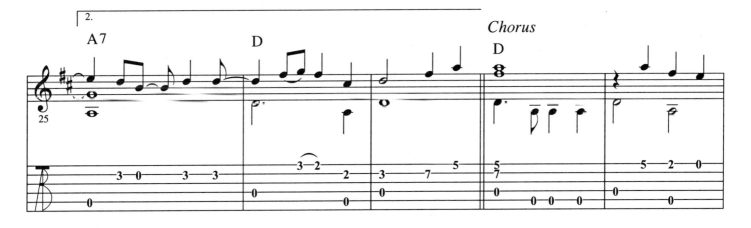

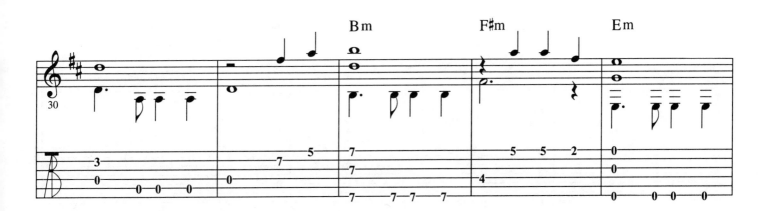

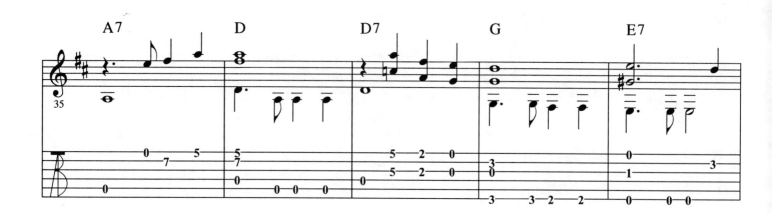

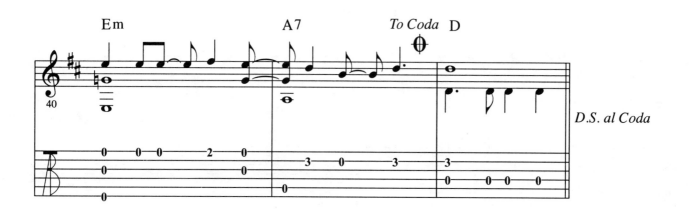

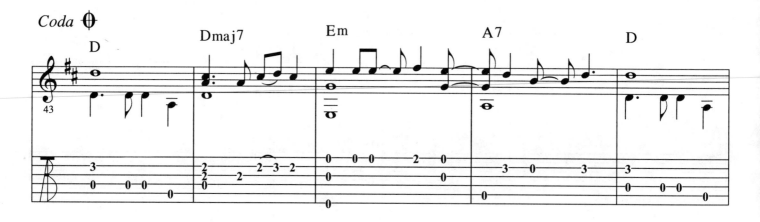

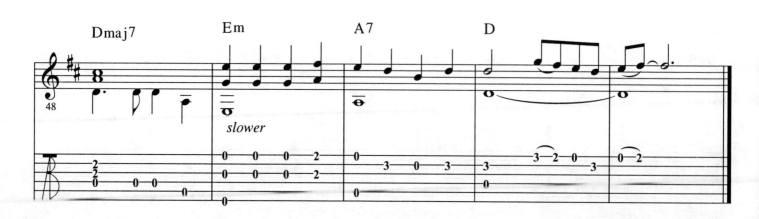

Oh, Pretty Woman

Words and Music by
Roy Orbison and Bill Dees
arranged for guitar by Steve Eckels

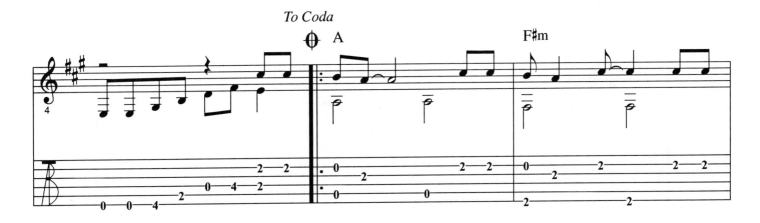

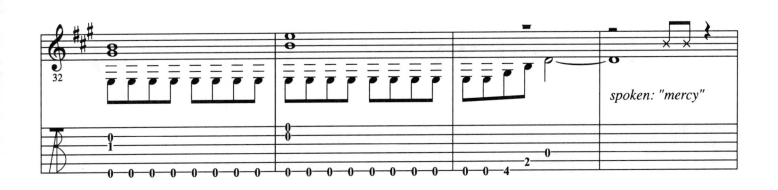

California Dreamin'

Words and Music by
John Phillips and Michelle Phillips
arranged for guitar by John Carlini

Repeat until Coda

Coda

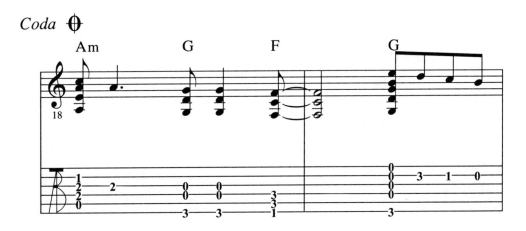

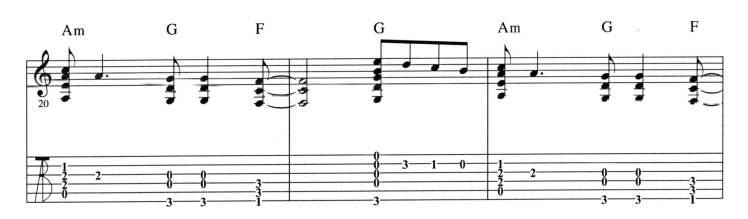

Desperado

Words and Music by
Don Henley and Glenn Frey
arranged for guitar by Mike Christiansen

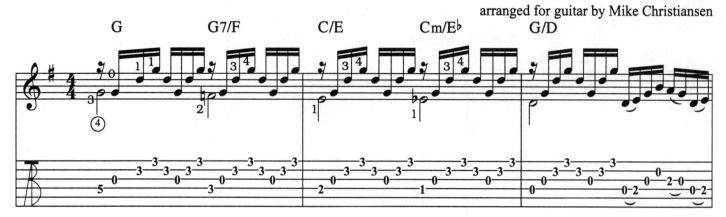

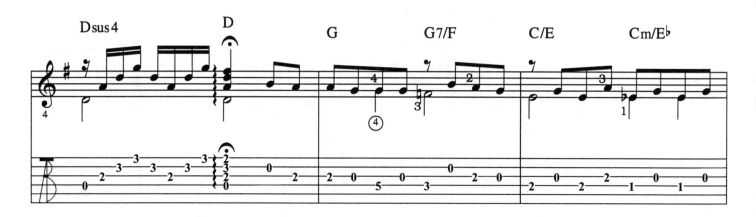

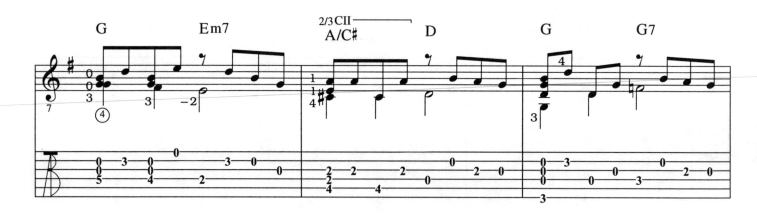

14

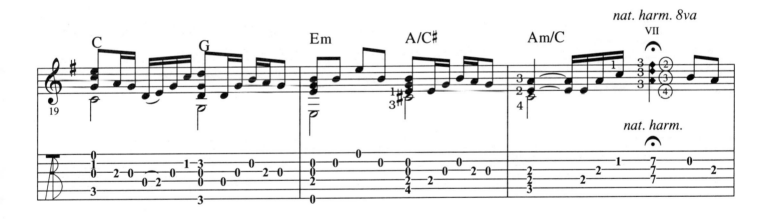
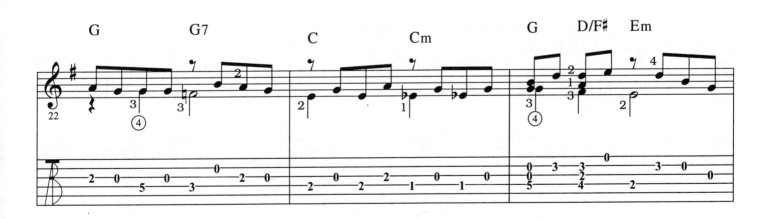

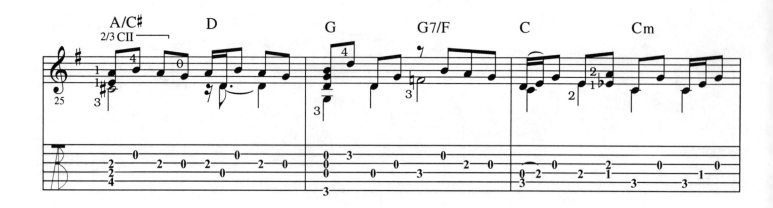

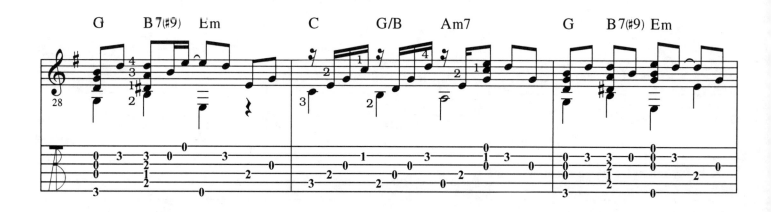

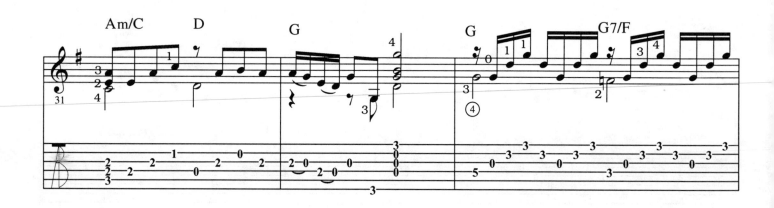

Hotel California

Words and Music by Don Henley,
Glenn Frey and Don Felder
arranged for guitar by Steve Eckels

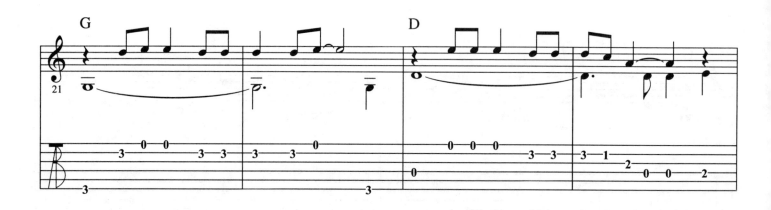

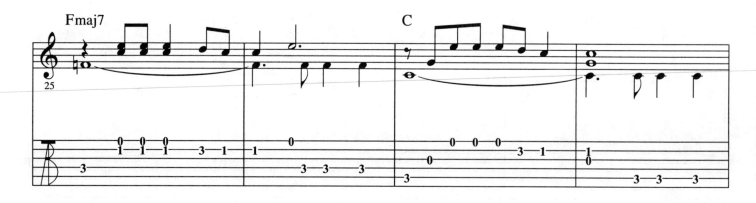

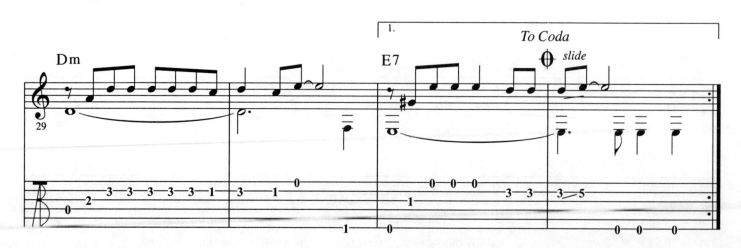

18

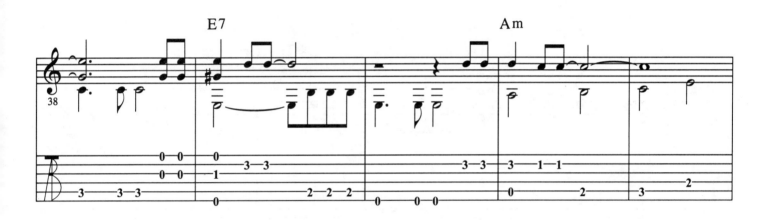

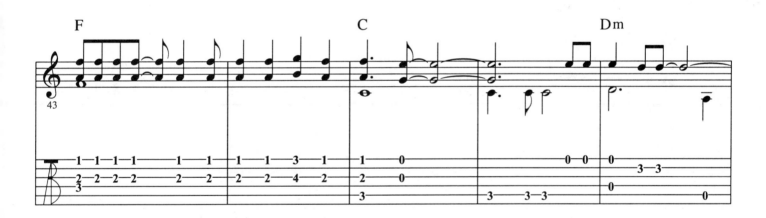

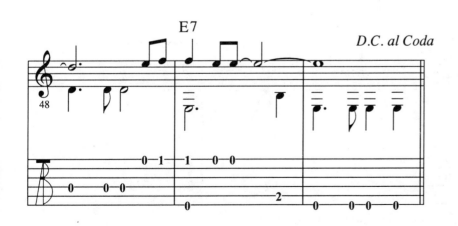

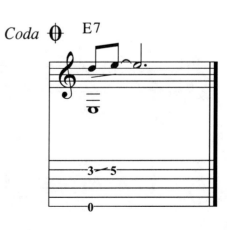

Killing Me Softly with His Song

by Norman Gimbel
and Charles Fox
arranged for guitar by Ole Halen

Bossa Nova

Layla

Words and Music by
Eric Clapton and Jim Gordon
arranged for guitar by Mike Christiansen

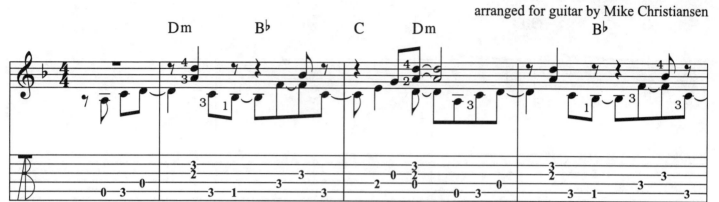

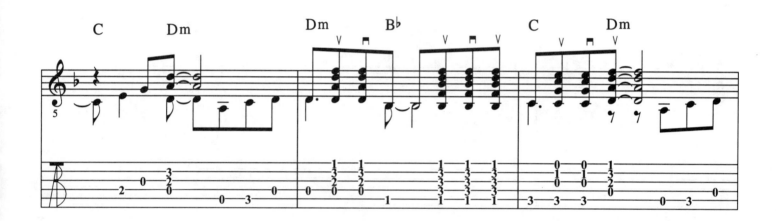

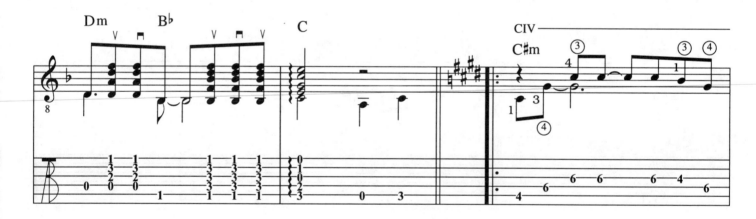

Mr. Bojangles

Words and Music by
Jerry Jeff Walker
arranged for guitar by John Carlini

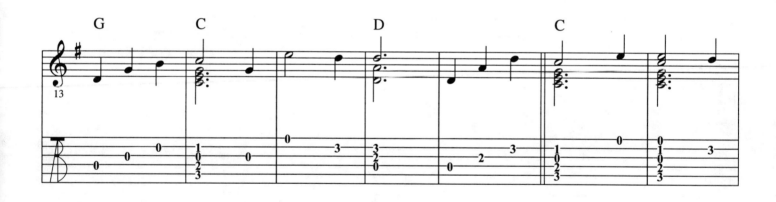

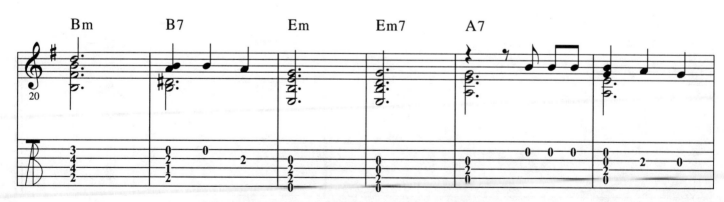

The Night They Drove Old Dixie Down

Words and Music by
Robbie Robertson
arranged for guitar by John Carlini

Verse

Proud Mary

Words and Music by
J. C. Fogerty
arranged for guitar by John Carlini

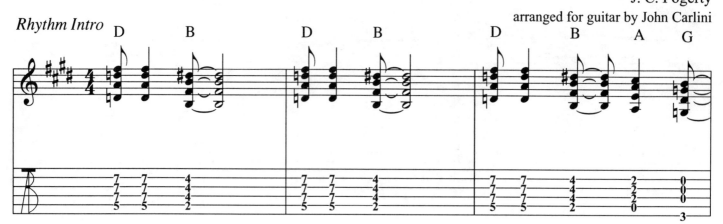

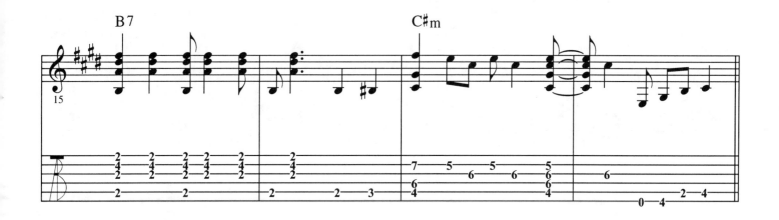

Chorus

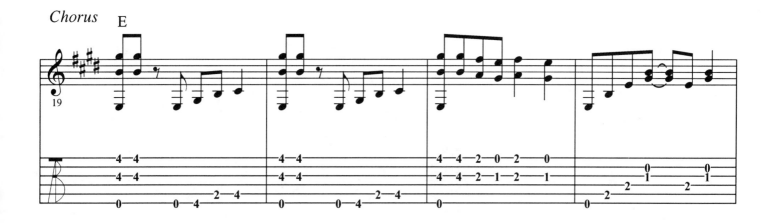

Rhythm Ending

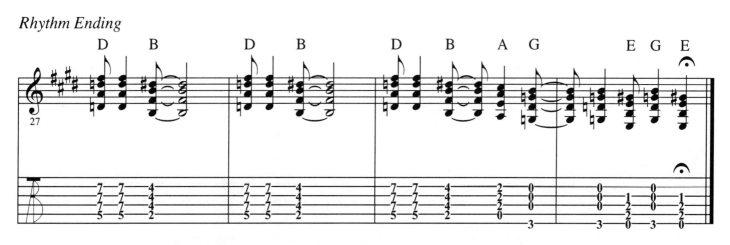

Tears in Heaven

Words and Music by
Eric Clapton and Will Jennings
arranged for guitar by Ole Halen

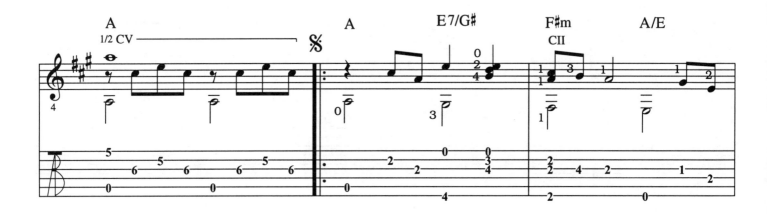

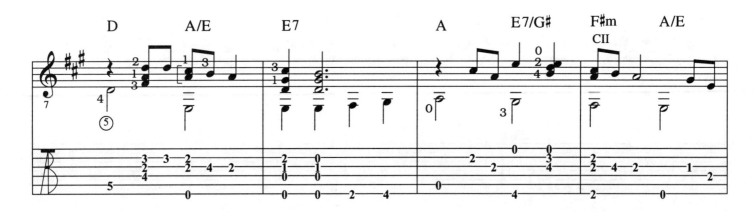

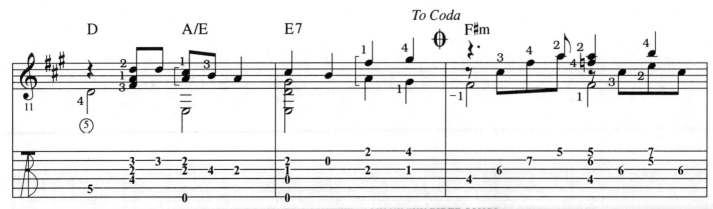

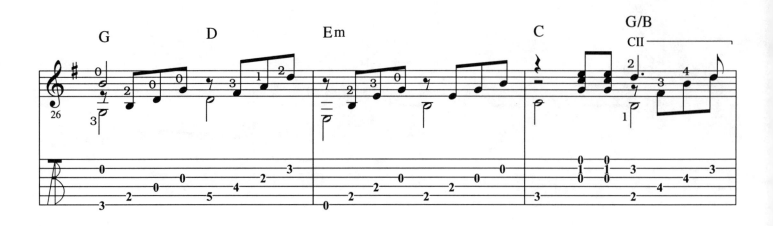

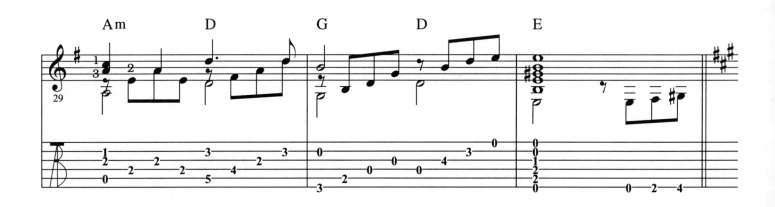

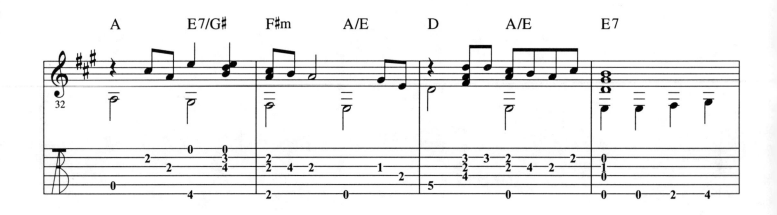

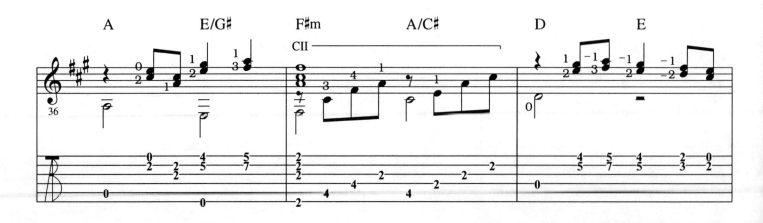

Vincent

(Starry, Starry Night)

Words and Music by
Don McLean
arranged for guitar by Ole Halen

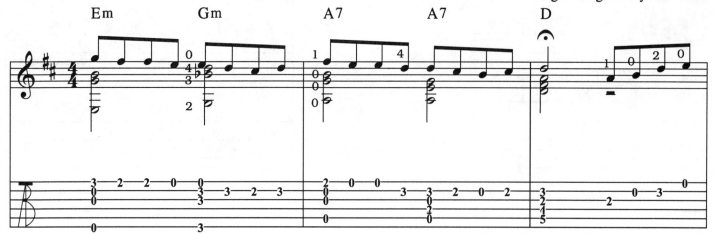

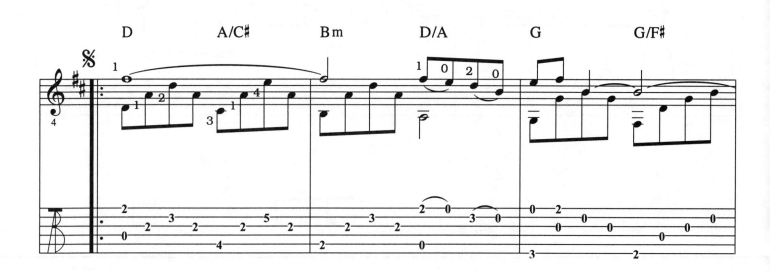

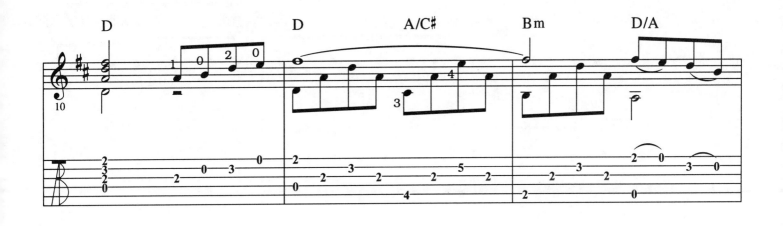

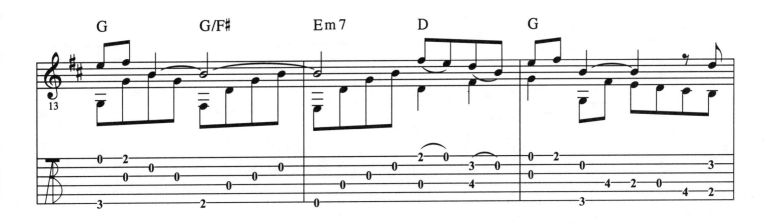

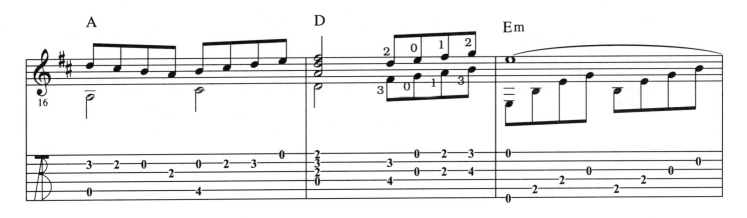

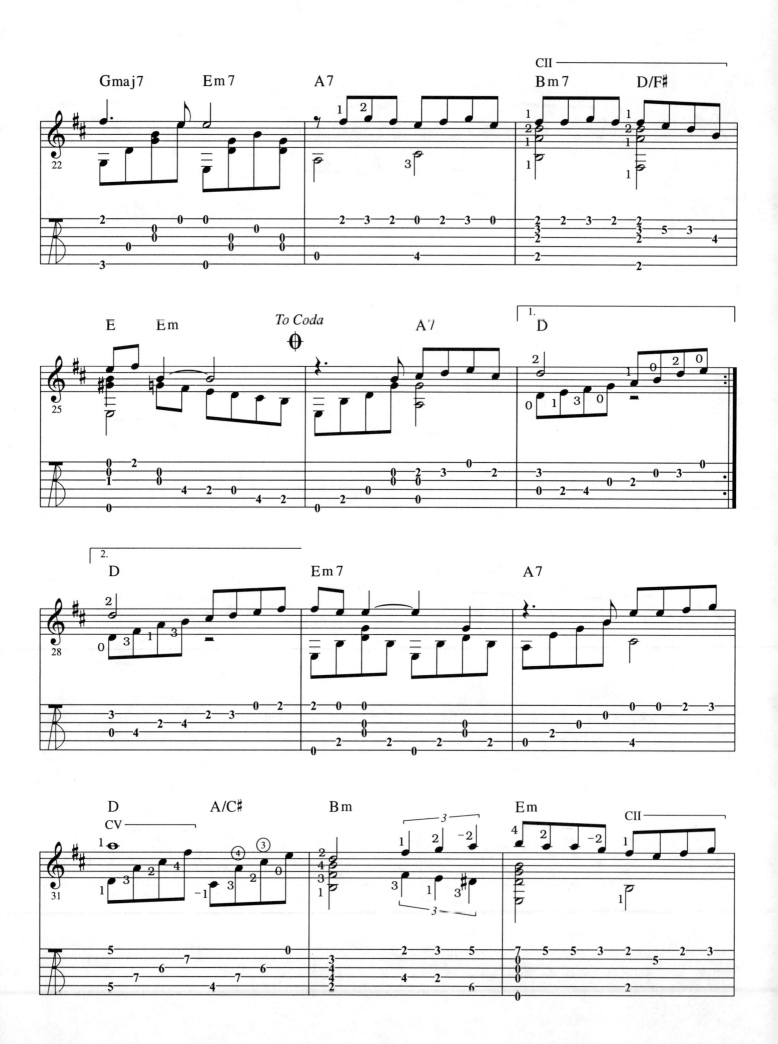

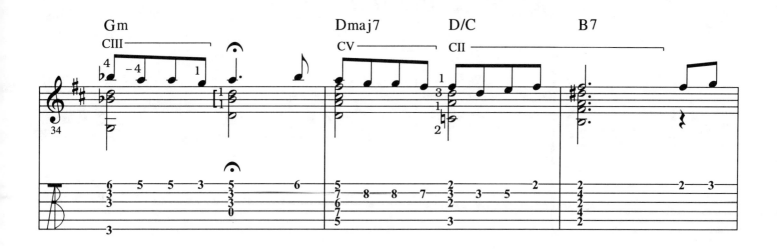

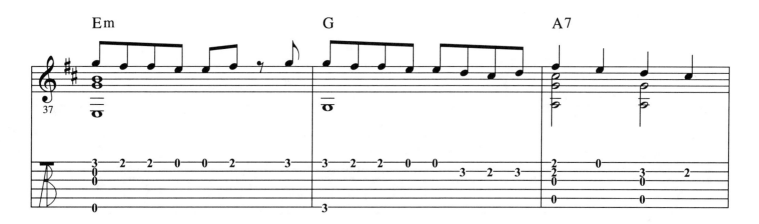

D.S. al Coda

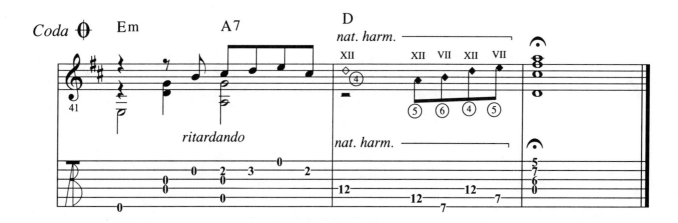

Wonderful Tonight

Words and Music
by Eric Clapton

arranged for guitar by Steve Eckels

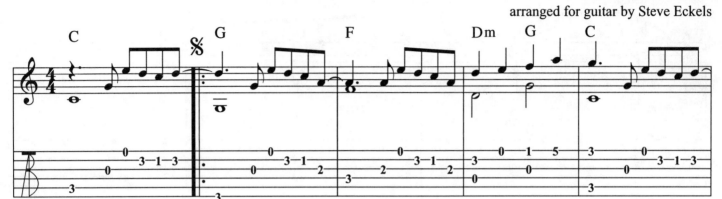

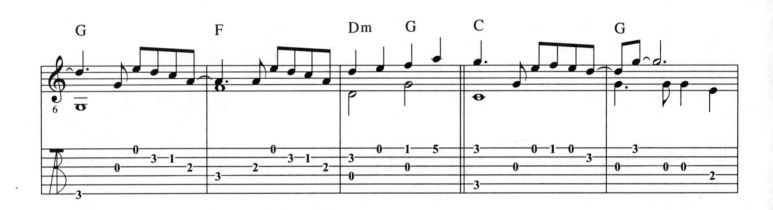

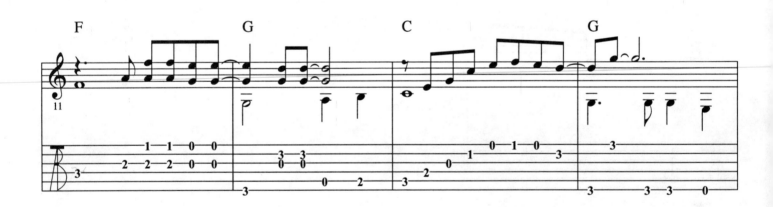

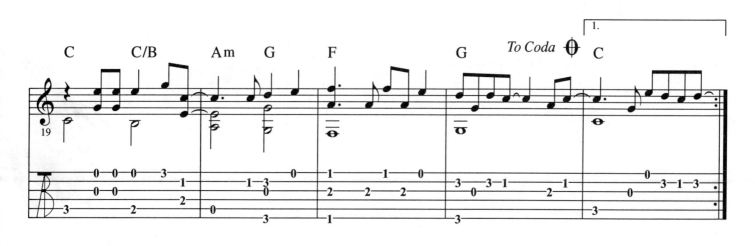

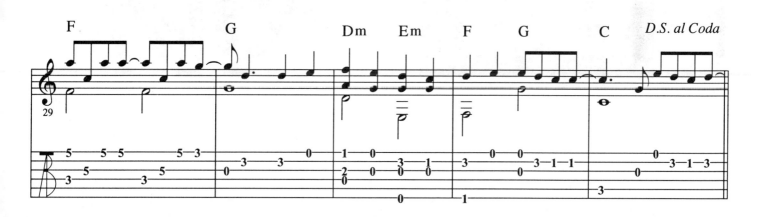

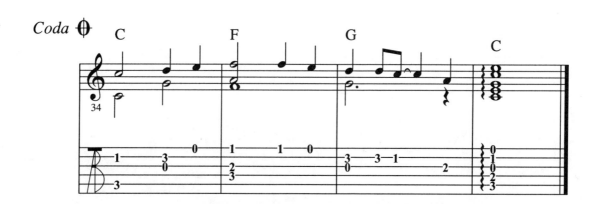